L
V
O
E.

Also by Atticus

The Truth About Magic
The Dark Between Stars
Love Her Wild

LVOE.

ATTICUS

Poems, Epigrams & Aphorisms

Andrews McMeel Publishing
a division of Andrews McMeel Universal
1130 Walnut Street, Kansas City, Missouri 64106

www.andrewsmcmeel.com

22 23 24 25 26 SDB 10 9 8 7 6 5 4 3 2 1

ISBN: 978-1-5248-7383-7

Library of Congress Control Number: 2022938925

Editor: Patty Rice
Art Director: Julie Barnes
Designers: Spencer Williams and Marissa Campeau
Production Editor: Elizabeth A. Garcia
Production Manager: Chadd Keim

About the TITLE:

A few years ago, I designed an engagement ring. It had two oval stones placed on a single gold band that together made an imperfect heart. I called the ring Coeur Parfait, which in French means perfect heart. *The idea being that love is two imperfect things coming together to make something beautiful. That's why I named this book* LVOE., *because even though love is imperfect, we all still see the beautiful.*

About the ART:

The art in this book was created by the world-famous tattoo artist Daniel Winter, also known as Winterstone. Each piece was inspired by a real tattoo.

I wrote this book on stolen time,
at parties, at work,
on trains and planes—
and I stole it all for you.

-Atticus

CHAPTERS

Words are but vague shadows of the volumes we mean.

–Theodore Dreiser

This book is for my forever girl.
For giving me a love
I didn't know could be true.

T.T

1.

HER

I loved her against reason, against promise,
against peace, against hope, against happiness,
against all discouragement that could be.

–Charles Dickens, Great Expectations

No matter what happens to us
from now
until the end
I want you to know
that I am certain of you
and you can be certain of that.

She had a rare gift
to bring out the best in people
to make them realize
they were so much more
than what they believed—
and that gift
I knew
was in all ways magic.

All she wanted
was for someone to look at her and see the person
she hid so well.

She came to me
in a light and smoky dawn
with a crown of white flowers
standing there in proud protest of the night
and the audacious rising of the sun
she swirled in sandalwood and incense
from far-off lands
whispering to me
in the secrets of the wind—
then as quickly as she came
she was gone
back into the coming of the day
daring me
to remember her forever
and that way she made me feel.

Who is this whose eyes
even now
sparkle through my mind
to steal pieces of my soul?
Her laugh ripples down my spine
with warm familiarity
as if
somehow
I'd spent a life with her already
as if the universe
had written this story years ago
and now sat atop high clouds
as it unfolded
smiling at my doubts—
as if there were any chance
I would not love this girl
for the rest of time.

FINDING HER
WAS REMEMBERING HER
FROM A THOUSAND
DIFFERENT DREAMS.

I learned quickly
it was never going to be
my side of the bed or hers
it was just all ours
and forever would be.

She was the kind of pretty
that was hard to kiss.

I'm powerless
to write
of the beauty
that I see
in the curl
of her lips
when she smiles
while she sleeps.

She left him
and for the first time
in a long time—
and maybe ever—
she was free.

I knew then
that all the meaning of life
existed somewhere
in this meadow
and this girl
with a butterfly on her finger.

I didn't see her beauty
I felt it
as plainly as the sun.

I wanted love
but not just any love
someone to look into my eyes
and see the truth of me
witness my pain
but also my hope
hold my soul
in their hands
and never let go—
I wanted that kind of love
and no other love
would do.

She was the dream
I had been waiting for—
the one to wake me up.

She had given up on love
or so she told herself
but
deep down inside
she was holding her breath
and clenching her fists
with the undying hope
that there was still
a little love
left to go.

He was the one who healed her—
who made her scars feel beautiful.

ACROSS A ROOM
TANGLED IN HER
IMAGINATION
THEY HAD SPENT
A LIFETIME TOGETHER
BEFORE
HE SAID
HELLO.

I built my home within her
it was never a choice really
one day
I just hung up my hat
took off my worn boots
and warmed myself
by the fire
crackling in her heart.

A million years of evolution
evolving you
to look this way
and evolving me
to love it so.

She wasn't
playing hard to get
she was just playing
tenderly
with a breakable heart.

That was her gift
she filled you with words
you didn't know were there.

Her whole life
flashed before her eyes
and it was
just as spectacular
as she remembered.

She was of witches and wolves
a wild and magical thing
impossible to hold
and harder to explain
and I was forever and always
under her spell.

You and I are stars
met once
in the blink of a universe
crossed only
for a moment
as the ebb and flow
of dust and atoms.

She kept going
for in her heart
she wanted to find out
what would happen
if she didn't give up
this time.

Whatever seed you are, bloom.

2.

LOVE

trust your heart
if the seas catch fire
(and live by love
though the stars walk backward)

–E. E. Cummings

"I love you more than chocolate," she said.
And I just wasn't ready
for that sort of pressure.

Love
is a language all its own
the ineffable blending of
sounds
smells
and sights
aligned in such a way
that it triggers in us
an infinite
truth.

So often
we find in love
all the things
we never realized
we were searching for.

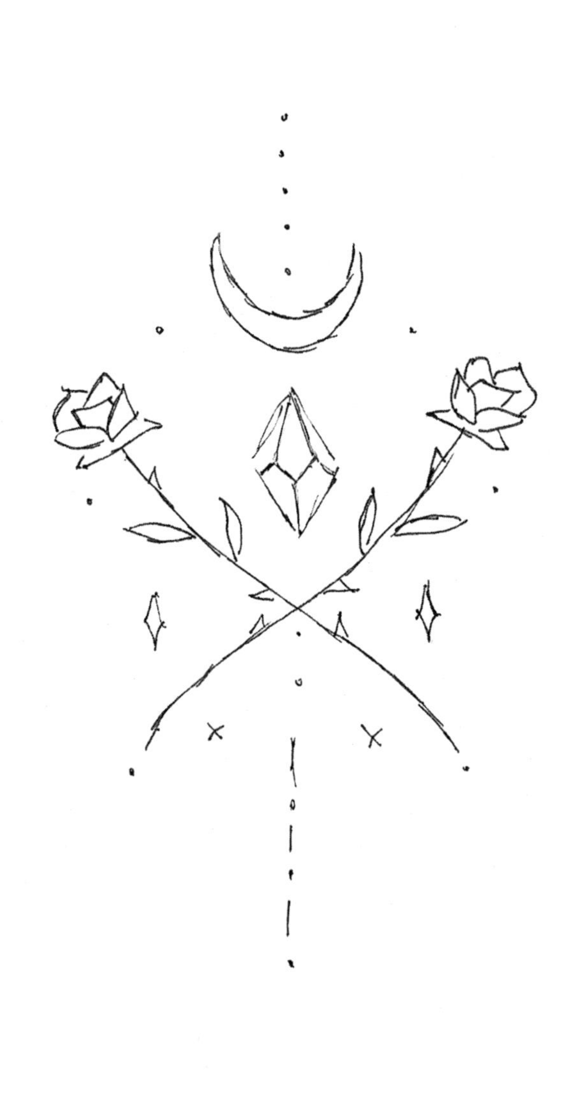

We must all learn
to love
or at least
die trying.

If only
I could begin
to forget
how deep
and much
I love you still.

Never forget
you're worth the love they are not giving.

Can we skip
the long beginning
and you just love me
from the start?

At the end of all time and space
in the black of all things left
I would like to think
there will still be
a remembrance
of love.

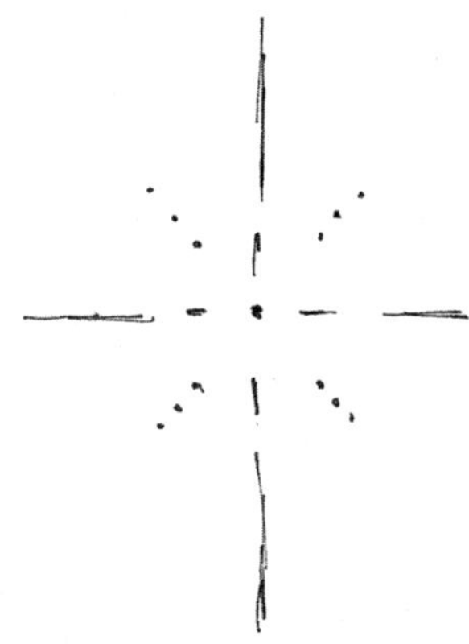

Beauty changes in love
it evolves
where at first you may find beauty on the outside
soon you find beauty everywhere else
in kindness, in trust, in safety
in hair sticking up in funny ways
in odd socks and stupid jokes—
beauty becomes
all the little things
that make our loves exactly who they are.

IF ONLY WE COULD FALL IN LOVE
WITH OURSELVES
AS EASILY AS WE FALL IN LOVE
WITH EVERYONE ELSE.

I loved her so intensely
words seemed unfit.
I needed to paint her
grab colors with my hands
and throw them at the wall.
There I would yell
"This is my love for you!"

The tombstone whispered
in its mossy breath
"Here lies a boy
who loved a girl."

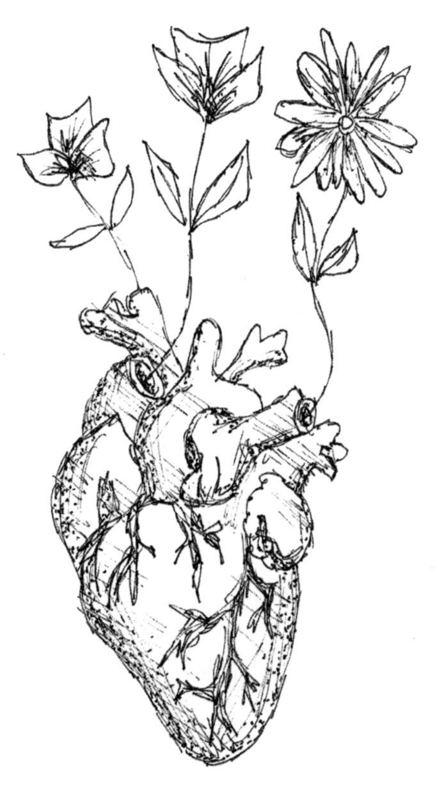

She wasn't scared
to walk away
she was scared
he wouldn't follow.

It's better
to be brave
and vulnerable
than safe
and all alone.

A thousand times
a day
I love you
a little more
than I did
the day before.

Love someone
like it's your very first night together
or your very last.

He said the one thing
she needed to hear
but never thought to hope for—
I believe in you completely.

I have always loved love—
love just doesn't seem to love me back.

True love exists in moments
stumbled upon
by accident
in hospitals
in airports
and underneath the stars
gone before you realize it was there
missed before you knew you had it.

I will never be perfect for you
but I will always imperfectly try to be.

How dare you
dare me
to dare
fall in love with you.

Love is here
and long away
in words and worlds unfolding
in lovers' arms and shooting stars
in old hands and sailing ships
in grassy hills and mountaintops
love is here
and long away
in words and worlds unfolding.

Our love
was as fragile
as the season's turning—
a crispy leaf
in the path of a toddler.

Life is the art
of sending memes
back and forth
with the people we love
until we die.

IT'S EASY TO LOVE SOMEONE
BEFORE YOU REALLY KNOW THEM
AND IT'S EVEN EASIER
AND HARDER
ONCE YOU DO.

Love is there for us
but also gone
whenever
we need it most.

If I'm being honest
it was a disturbingly short
amount of time
between meeting you
and wanting to say
"I love you."

Love is a wondrous and wild storm
we must—
while we can—
dance in the rain.

I will be
forever haunted
by the memories
of you
they wander
the empty
hallways
of my soul—
opening doors
and knocking
things off tables.

Love is—
late-night
kissing at stoplights
after the lights
have turned green.

Don't love someone
only to be loved back
love to love them
unselfishly
honestly.
Only then
can you truly
be in love.

Love is not something to be found
it is something to be built
brick by careful brick
and the more carefully
it is built
the stronger it will be
for when life's winds blow
and storms shake the walls.

Love knows no distance
but it prefers snuggling.

Be twice as powerful as you think you are.

It's hard to be in love
and to be vulnerable
you must open the door
to that secret and high-walled
garden of your soul
that you have always kept
so carefully locked—
for so many years—
and then let another person inside
hoping and praying
they don't break anything.

I've loved you
since the first day
I learned to love.
You were the face
I saw in my dreams
the girl I drew in art class
and kept crumpled
in my pocket—
I knew you were out there
and so I waited
patiently
for you to walk into my life
one summer
in Rome.

Don't dream to live forever
dream to forever live
while you're alive.

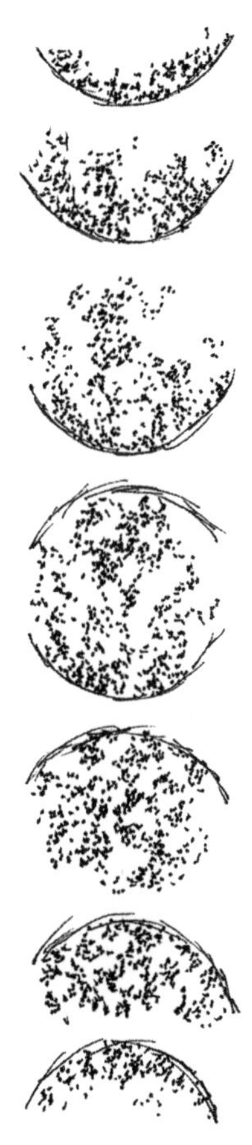

I promise
to spend
the rest of my forever
painting you
with words.

The answer
to the question
"Are you in love?"
should be simple
and if it's not
then it is.

Remembering that it all ends soon
isn't a bad thing
it frees us
to live as we should
with lots of love
and little worry.

Young love is about loving the ones who leave you—
old love is about loving the ones who never would.

NO GREAT LOVE
WAS PERFECT
NO GREAT LOVE
WASN'T BRAVELY
FOUGHT FOR.

There is a moment
in some girls' lives
when they put on a dress
for the very first time
and walk into the world
feeling more beautiful
than they ever have
and ever will again.
And somewhere—
I like to think—
Audrey Hepburn smiles.

3.

WANDER

And the ashes blew towards us
with the salt wind from the sea.

–Daphne du Maurier, Rebecca

We dangled our legs off Pont Neuf bridge
smoked cigarettes we rolled
and drank wine without labels—
time stood still for us
there were no thoughts of future or past
just the burning now
and we reveled in it—
endless days
on the banks of
endless rivers
with cloudless skies
and youth to burn.

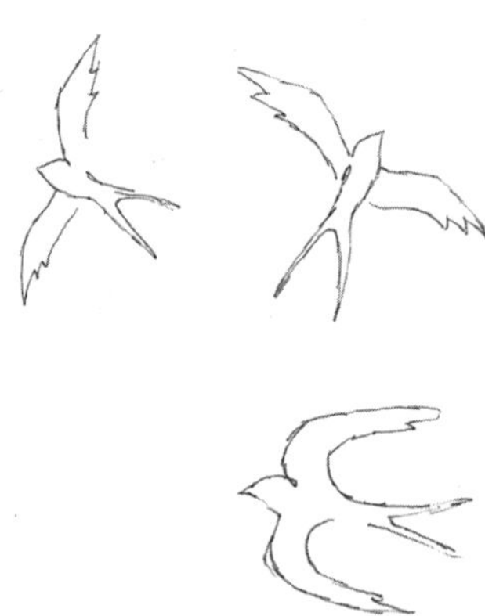

Nothing
will forget him faster
than a bottle of rosé
and quickly
embarked
adventure.

We must all find the courage to follow
the path that's lit up in our hearts.

Paris knew love
better than I
ever could
so I let the city
take her hand
and followed
close behind
picking up the pieces
of her
melting heart.

We shared a journal, remember?
You would draw
and I would write
and together we would wander
the streets of Paris
drunk on the idea of it all
and the rosé—
we weren't the first to love there
nor would we be the last
but something of our love
I hoped
would live on forever
soaked deep within those cobblestones
and the bleeding ink of time.

NOSTALGIA
IS THAT HAPPY-SAD WAY
OF LOOKING BACKWARD
IN SEPIA.

Never go in search of love
go in search of life
and life will find you
the love you seek.

Life is a great and wondrous dream
as great and wondrous
as we can possibly dream.

What a shame it would be
to see only what is real in this world.

So many of us
spend our lives
in our minds
wandering from past to future
like weary time travelers
completely ignoring
the beautiful now
unraveling all around us.

So many kisses, so little time.

There is a place I know
a garden in a forest
where the trees have parted
enough to let the light in
and the flowers to grow—
in a meadow with walls of trees on every side
and a mossy floor
where the flowers pour through
and the dust rises to mix with the sun's rays
and sparkle beams up to the blues of sky
where a single bird flies alone.
This place is you within me.
It is my home.

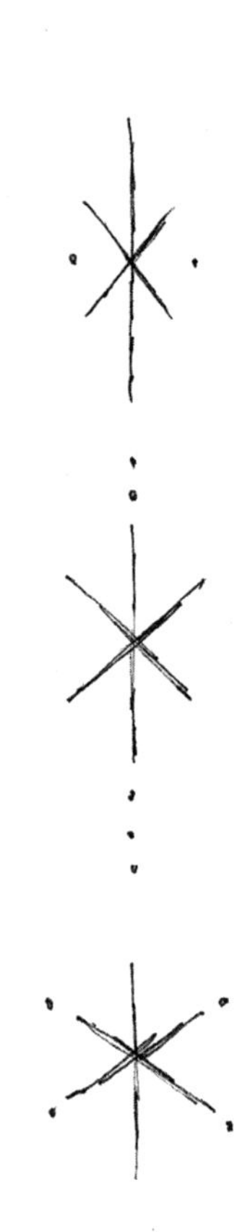

We are all just
the ghosts of stars
shining our little shine
back to the sky.

We will always have Paris
she said
and she was right
our love
had lived and died
in the gentle to and fro
of a city's beating heart.

It began to rain
and the streetlights
twinkled
off the old stones
like tinsel on a Christmas tree
and we danced
in the empty streets
to the symphony
of the changing traffic lights
knowing life
would never
be the same.

Walk toward the good in life and one day you will arrive.

Embark today
on the grand adventure
that is
the rest of your life.

It was in that moment
when I was finally
comfortable with being alone
that you
wandered into my life
demanding snuggles.

My only company
was the endless canvas of stars
and my boots
the ink dabs
on dusty parchment
unrolling toward
the horizon.

In the mornings
we'd sip coffee
and I'd write as the sun rose
over the rolling hills of cypress trees and vines.
We'd walk the Roman pathways
down to the lake
through the olive tree groves
and ancient ash forests
to the stream and banks of the vineyards.
There, we'd eat grapes off the vines
and spit their seeds into the dirt.
We'd rest under the old oak tree
and listen to the crickets' buzz
and the otherwise silence of the hills.
A hawk
would float on the currents above
as effortless as we were.
And as the sun set, we'd sip our wine
knowing this was life as life intended
somewhere in this Tuscan dream.

I loved you once
in a swimming pool in France
it was summer and it rained
I looked at you
and loved you then
I never told you
but it's true
I loved you
and us
and the chance of all things
and even though
it didn't last
I will always love
that day I loved you.

We floated down French rivers
on a boat pushed by steam
passed rolling hills and vineyards
baked by the sun.
Wine is stored sunlight, Galileo said.
The crickets sang to us
as we'd walk to old churches
that smelled like old stone
where light sprinkled through stained glass
in melancholies of muted paints
dancing around our footprints.
I'd write poems and ideas in a little black book—
I want to see the world with you, I wrote.
You drew the rooftops
and took pictures of wooden doors—
then we'd walk to little towns
down little Roman paths.
"This is heaven," I thought.
Every heaven is different,
but this is mine—
we'd drink wine at old cafés
and espresso in tiny cups
we'd buy cheese and bread and walk the fields
to the old oak trees always in the middle

where we'd eat our snack and a loaf of bread
we got for a euro.
I thought of my grandfather
and the hot days where I grew up—
I'll try not to die as young, I wrote—
and as the fireflies began to sparkle
we'd walk back to our boat before it left
and *I promised,* I wrote
to always remember this
and the heaven I'd see again.

Destiny came knocking at my doorstep
and to be honest
she was rather rude.

I lost my way
all the way to you
and in you
I found
all the way
back
to me.

4.

SOUL

I wish you to know that you have been
the last dream of my soul.

–*Charles Dickens,* A Tale of Two Cities

The ones we've loved
are never really gone
not really
they come back to us forever after
in songs
in sunsets
and Sundays in the rain.

I'm sorry
we fell out of love.
I am.
The truth is
we didn't love the same
and it's not your fault
and it's not mine
it's just the truth—
and that
my love
is why I'm sorry.

Don't give them years
if they won't give you a lifetime.

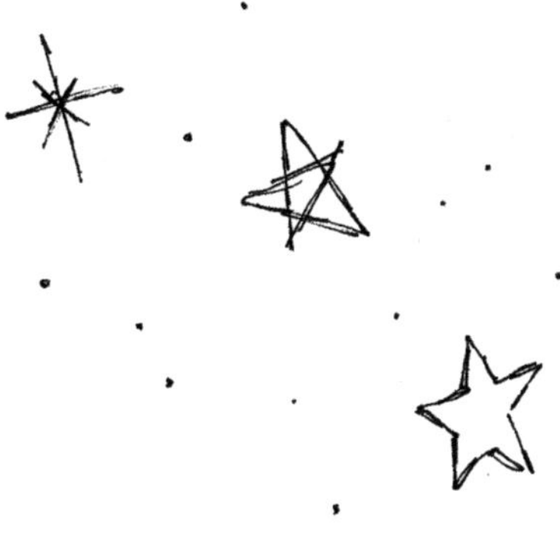

You are all the ways
my soul likes to dream.

When I die
I want to fall into my bed exhausted
covered in scars
stories buzzing in my head
of memories and inside jokes
from a lifetime of misadventure—
my broken bones barely healed
my skin weathered and hair matted
a body running on fumes
and I want to lie there
in a room full of grandchildren
minds alive with curiosity
for a world begging to be explored
with a beautiful wife
with soft hands in mine
who will look at me
and smile
because she knows me best
and as I go
she will squeeze my hand
stories sparkling in my eyes
as I leave
on one last adventure.

Many of us
are extremely uncomfortable
being happy
like wearing someone else's clothes
so much so
that we quickly
destruct any happiness that finds us
to return
to the comfortable agony
we know so well.

Sometimes
friends
are the only escape
we have from ourselves.

Our story wasn't over yet
not yet
our souls
still had a few more dances
left to go.

THERE IS NOTHING
SO BRAVE
IN THE WHOLE WIDE WORLD
AS A CANDLE
PERSISTING
TO LIVE ON
IN THE WIND.

Smile
and let go
it's just life after all
and you're doing
it right
just by living.

There is a great miracle
that occurs when we listen
to that little voice inside our heads
that tells us truthfully
who we are and why.

Many don't realize
that some of us
wage
a great battle
every day
just to feel normal.

Imagine we all had the courage to be
the strange
and wondrous creatures
we were born to be.

Life is the art
of pretending to be normal.

I once dreamed a dream
I was the last person on Earth
charged with saying goodbye
to the end of the human race
watching lastly
our kingdoms fade—
saying goodbye
to the trees
to the clouds
to all the ways we've come
and the loves we've been
to the wars we've fought
and the cities we've built.
I am the last
the last to fade
beside this tree
on a hill
blowing in the wind
not sad
even smiling.
What a stand
what a stand we made
and this is where it ends
and too where we began
as a pure white light.

So, in that gentle breeze
beside that gentle tree
I smile brightly
and say goodbye
one last time
as we fade
back into the dust of it all.

Stay in the light
the old man said
and you'll always
find the way.

You are
the series of mistakes
that needed to happen
for you to find your you.

We are all human
alone and together
surviving
in the lonely kingdoms of ourselves.

What if you were already
the incredible person
you're pretty sure you could be?

Deep down
she didn't believe
she deserved to be loved
or to be happy
and so she did
what she always did
when she got scared
she drove him back
away from her darkness
away from her chaos—
but unlike the others
he didn't go
he had seen the truth of her
burning deep inside
and he would never give up now
not until she became
that wonderful light
he saw so deep within.

She didn't ask
the world to be happy
she only asked
not to be
so sad.

Time fights always
for the broken hearts.

Be yourself.
Someone out there loves
the person
you're pretending not to be.

Never make
the same mistake
twice—
unless
of course
he makes
you laugh.

The broken heart is twice shy.

I'VE LOST
YOU
AND WILL
LIVE ON
FOREVER NOW
IN A
DWINDLED DAWN
WITHOUT
YOU.

She knew it was over
when she felt alone in his arms.

She fell
into the
gentle lullaby
of old age—
like a great
and tender
dimming
of a well-burned star.

The wind stirred the leaves with a breeze
as it always did before the weather turned.
It was the end of the summer once more.
The rains of fall were coming.
We'd come back to this cabin of our youth again
but it would never be the same.
We were growing up, getting married, having kids.
We'd never again be the same carefree children
building forts and running through the shell trails to the sea.
And as we closed the cabin down and said goodbye
it made me sad to think
it was goodbye
to summer and to youth.
They floated away that day
on the cool fall breeze.

Strong is the soul that is beaten but unbroken.

It's one of life's great tragedies
to love someone
only after they are gone.

It's easy to forget sometimes
that somewhere
before
all the hate
all the tears
and all the heartbreak
there was
in the beginning—
love.

THE HARDEST PART
OF LOSING YOU
WAS LOSING THE DREAMS
WE DREAMED TOGETHER.

I walk beside the river
lapping in the spangled shade of willows—
you are with me again
aren't you?
I wonder
is your daydream in heaven
the same as mine?
Are you this ghost I walk beside?
I hold your hand
and know you are.

The greatest gift
she ever gave
was to let him go—
off to new adventures
to new travels
to maybe even
one day new love—
and as impossible as it was
she knew it was right—
for deep within
she held hope
that one day
a person she once loved
could be happy.

Here
in your arms
is where I shall grow old.

I told her I was lost in this world
and she smiled
because she was too.
We were all lost somehow
but we didn't care.
We had
in the chaos
found each other.

There will always be magic in the world
as long as there are
fireflies
shooting stars
and love
in a little girl's heart.
I left my heart in Paris
in the forgetful fingers
of a Parisian princess.
I'm sure it will be gone by the time I return
left in a café somewhere
lost amongst empty glasses of champagne
cigarettes burning in ashtrays
and the cologne of a tall painter
with bad hair and interesting ideas
lingering on the still, smoky air.

I felt in her
a great
and longing sadness
I wanted to wrap her in a blanket
and tell her she was safe forever
and so I did
and so I prayed she would be.

Everything
we've
built and loved
are sandcastles
in the tide.

We are all worth loving
sometimes we just need
someone to take a chance on us.

She left him—
and began
on that day
a long-overdue
adventure within.

I have a theory
that all poets
are lost souls
wandering
their way back
to Paris.

He had stolen her yesterdays
but not her tomorrows
those were hers
and one by one
she stole them back.

5.

CUDDLE

And the rest is rust and stardust.

–Vladimir Nabokov, Lolita

Sometimes I wrestle my demons.
Sometimes we just cuddle.

The hummingbirds
never came on Sundays.
Every day they'd come
a hundred times a day they'd come
but not on Sundays
and I always wondered
where they went.
Maybe they were like me
worried of Mondays—
and I always wished I could go
where the hummingbirds
went on Sundays.

Vellichor
means
"the strange wistfulness
of used bookshops"—
and
it makes me smile to think
that such a word was thought
important enough
to exist.

If I met her in a cave
in the dark
where no light ever lived
she would still be
the brightest flame I'd ever seen
for it was always the way she was
never the way she looked
that made her beautiful to me
and beautiful she was
for it was only when I closed my eyes
and stood there
in that darkest cave
that she truly
blinded me
with beauty.

A smile is a powerful thing
that must be wielded carefully—
a girl smiles at a boy at a bus stop
never to think about it again
but the boy
will never forget
he will think about it often and forever
for years and years to come
until even at the end
on his deathbed
he will remember her again—
that girl
who smiled at him once
at a bus stop.

She
had him
always
in her
closed
eyes.

Take my soul
but make good poetry of it.

Hurry up, she said—
let's grow old together.

Never
neglect
a kiss
or a sunset.

WE ARE ALL MADE
OF LIGHT AND DARK
FIGHTING GREAT BATTLES
THROUGH THE DUSK.

There was a storm in her soul
rocky seas from a hundred stormy nights
but there was also light
warm winds
from a distant shore
so that's where I headed
toward the light
that shone in her eyes.

I have noticed
that in every photo
taken of us
we are either kissing
or about to
and I think that's
a beautiful truth about us.

Poetry
is the place
where two
imaginations
touch.

Time is all we have and don't.

How do you write
the things you do?
She asked.
Hard work
and discipline.
I said.
Coffee
and cigarettes.
I thought.

When I was young
and my parents fought
my little sister
would get scared
so I'd make up stories for her
to take us away to
happier places.
I think that's all my poetry is
making up stories
for all of us who are scared
to take us away
to happier places.

Life is too short
not to always pretend
you're magnificent.

You were
all things to me
but you were also good
and I loved
that good about you—
in this
so dark a world
it was
so rare a thing.

The poet waits patiently
to paint the unsaid.

Every word I write
is a breath
that keeps
me alive.

My dad died today
she said.
He is gone
and you know what
it made me realize?
That so much of life doesn't matter
all of this
all the money
the cars
the work
no one's keeping score
no one cares at the end.
We are all just an inch away from death–
the only things that matter
are love and friendship
and being a good person
the best we can be
but not perfect
never perfect
and the most important thing
is letting go
of all these little things
that we think mean so much.
The drama, the stresses.
None of it matters.

I know that today.
I see it so clearly.
Death makes us see things clearly.
And do you know the sad part?
I'm going to forget this feeling soon
and so are you
and that's the beautiful and tragic part about
forgetting.

To love and be loved is the true poetry of life.

Poetry found me
where love
had left me
young and all alone.

EVERYTHING THAT WAS
AND IS
AND EVER WILL BE
IS WITHIN YOU.

We were
endlessly
carelessly
hopelessly
in love
and the rest
was just the details.

I stumbled upon myself in you.

LOVE HER, BUT LEAVE HER WILD

The boy ran
quick as rain
through grassy fields awake in dew
in moon-dipped steps
a summer's night—
through fireflies
and sparkling stars
a glass jar in hand
his little cloud breaths
up to the open sky—
and there
there at once
alone in that summer field, she flew
a fairy shining
as bright as day
and the stars, once bright
dimmed back in crimsons
jealous of the way she shone
she, the brightest light he'd ever seen
so bright she burned, for she loved him too
and he put her gently in his hands
and placed her in the jar
his love
within his coat.
Back to the town, he ran
a thousand laughs caught in his throat

everything he loved
was finally his
and there, with all the people's eyes around
he brought the jar out from his robes
and held it high above
his shining prize
for all to see—
but, alas
she was dim
and though she tried
she could not shine so brightly
and the boy's heart fell
and the people turned away and laughed.
"But I love her," he said.
"More than anything I could ever love.
Why can't she shine for the world?"
And the old man in the corner
beckoned the boy close
to whisper something in his ear.
The boy looked up and back at his fairy—
dimming in the glass.
He nodded at the man
for he knew the old man's words were true
and with tears in his eyes
sparkling like diamonds he ran
faster than he'd ever run

the wind tearing his eyes ever more—
back through the moonlit steps
through the darkened grass
through the fireflies
and shimmering stars—
and there
in that summer field, alone
he opened up the glass once more
and held it to the sky
and his love, his fairy, flittered out—
tenderly, brightly
she began to burn again
even brighter than before
and as he cried
and loved her so
the old man's words
echoed in his mind—
love her
he said
but leave her wild.

Stay young,
stay brave,
stay wild.

xx Atticus